Speech Therapy for 0–5-Year-Olds

Discover if your child's communication skills are delayed and how you can help improve their understanding, talking and play skills with 73 games created by a speech and language therapist

Speech and Language Therapist

Helen Oakmoor

Please consult a licensed professional before attempting any techniques outlined in this book.

By reading this document, the reader agrees that under no circumstances is the author responsible for any losses, direct or indirect, which are incurred as a result of the use of the information contained within this document, including, but not limited to, errors, omissions, or inaccuracies.

Dedication

I want to dedicate this book to my children. I want to say that I love you all very much and I know you will do great things in your lives! I am already, immensely proud, of all of you for being such wonderful human beings!

I also want to give a special mention to my precious little 'great niece' who was late with her talking. Her mum was so worried and anxious about her delayed talking and wondered if she would ever talk properly. Both mother and daughter inspired me to write this book to help them both and many other parents who might be in the same situation.

By the way, she is a little chatterbox now!

Table of Contents

A GIFT for You

Do not start this book without accessing the FREE resources which will help you get the most out of this book!

1. Parents' Self-Rating Chart
2. Daily Child's Play Progress Record Chart
3. A List of First 100 Words Children Learn

Click the link below to get the resources and start implementing the advice.

https://helenoakmoor.activehosted.com/f/25

Introduction

How would you feel if you were told you can help your child flourish in language and communication with a few minutes a day of play time? You don't need to spend a fortune. In fact, it can be done with everyday objects you find in your home. Sounds too good to be true, right?

Five Minutes a Day! It's nothing; we probably spend more time checking emails or cleaning up the toys. Nevertheless, those five minutes are invaluable. This is the minimum time you should spend 'teaching' early interaction skills to your child. It is important to begin by saying that the strategies we are going to learn are for helping typically developing children. However, they can also be used with children who have special needs. You may need to adapt your language and the level of difficulty of the play activity you are trying to match with the abilities of your child, but we will work on this together.

We are going to talk about the strategies you need to try to help your child develop their speech, language and play skills. These strategies are easy to follow and

1

implement in your daily routines with your child. Whether you are at home or out and about, all you need is a minimum of five minutes a day. Hopefully, over time, you will be motivated and become more confident, and your child will be keen to join in the play activities with you. I am sure you will find that you are spending much more than just five minutes practising these skills.

I understand the anxiety and concern you may have for your child, as I see this almost every day of my working week. As parents, we want our children to be well behaved, use language to ask for what they want and to understand what we are saying to them.

Maybe your child is starting nursery/kindergarten soon and you want them to settle in quickly and be able to communicate effectively with their teachers. You want your child to be able to play appropriately and share toys with their peers. Understandably, you want your child to be able to follow the adult-led activities at home and in the nursery, which helps them to learn.

We aren't talking about those jaw-dropping moments when your child says or does something and you wish the ground would swallow you up. Little people are brutally honest and this is part of growing up. We are talking about strategies that will help children to form the correct sounds so that they are understood. To string together the right grammatical sentences that they may otherwise have difficulties with.

Family and friends can unintentionally make life a little more difficult by making comments like 'you must have your hands full with Jack', or 'I don't know how you manage with Lilly', referring to your child who has a short attention span or has not yet learned to share their toys with others. They mean well with their advice, but it certainly doesn't help.

As parents, we are told not to compare our children to other children in our friends and family circle, as every child is an individual and has their own developmental path. Having said that, I can understand how difficult it is not to compare, when your friend's child can have a mini-conversation with their parent and your little boy has only a few single words at the same age. And I'm sure we all know at least one parent who revels in showing off their child's communicative skills. Being a parent myself, I understand why this would be frustrating and worrying for you.

You have made the right decision to try and help your child to develop their skills. I have put together strategies to help your child with their early interaction and play skills, whether you feel they need help because they are not at the same level as other children at the same age, or you just want some simple fun activities to do with your child even if they are absolutely on target with their development.

Start implementing these strategies and you will see the difference in your child over a short time. Spending time with your child practising social interaction can not only teach them the necessary skills but also build a positive relationship with you, which you will cherish. BUT remember to be consistent with practice (minimum five minutes daily), the more you practise, the better the results.

In this book, I will give you a list of 73 games to target the areas of delay and these will help you to support your child. These strategies will become second nature to you. You will have all the activities for each area of development at your fingertips. You will learn to adapt to work on the different areas of development whether you are at home, in the car, at the park, or in the restaurant.

This book gives you strategies to practise, starting with newborn babies to children up to five years old. You're going to learn how to use these tips and tricks so you will never have to worry about your child's communication skills again.

You will learn what we mean by 'early interaction skills and play'. You will learn to recognize the delay in your child's development, as you will be provided with ages and stages of each developmental area. You will learn what to look for to determine if your child has a delay in their early development and if so, how you can help to bridge that gap, or when and where to seek professional help, if required.

You will be given lots of ideas for activities that you can put together at home or wherever you are to engage with your child. You do not need to go out and spend lots of money and buy equipment or toys. Use what you already have at home.

You will be given strategies on how you can help your child in each chapter. Instead of just listing activities, I want you to be able to get the most out of each idea I provide. For this reason, these ideas will also include tips on how to prepare your child and the environment before starting any activity when targeting a skill at home. The activities and games are listed in the last chapter for each stage of development, where you can quickly access them.

A bit About the Author

I have a bachelor of science (hons) clinical language sciences: speech and language therapy degree. I have been working as a speech and language therapist for over two decades with children between 1 and 16 years old, and I must say I think I have the most amazing job in the world.

Working with children who have a wide range of issues on a one-to-one basis, e.g., with speech, language, and communication delay in varying degrees, and with children with hearing difficulties, has given me a wealth of knowledge and experience that I am keen to share with you.

I have learnt to appreciate how different each and every child is, thanks to having worked with children of mixed abilities, from something simple and easily supported as delayed attention and listening skills, speech, and language delay/disorder, to children with a diagnosis of autism who require a differential curriculum in school.

Working closely with other professionals such as health visitors, physiotherapists, consultant paediatricians, teachers, headteachers and special education needs coordinators has given me insight and valuable experience into how we make sure that the child is at the centre of everything, and that we work together to help put in place all the possible support required by the child and their family.

If you are first-time parents and feel unsure about how you should be helping your child to develop their early skills, or you are parents of children who are not yet communicating at the level their older siblings were at the same age, and you want some ideas on how to help them, then this is the book for you.

Are you ready to help your child to improve their early interaction skills? Keep reading.

Chapter 1

A Brief Discussion on the Psychology of Child Development

I can feel the eyes rolling as some may wonder, 'Why start with the psychology of child development?' I know you want to get straight on to the juicy strategies and start seeing the difference. I like to start here because it often clears up misconceptions that people have read and it also helps to become more familiar with key people who have developed the techniques we will discuss. It's also quite interesting to see just how far research has come in the last century, which gives us hope about what is still to come.

Let's begin with a brief look at child developmental psychology, to learn how children develop their communication skills. Research in this area started in the early 1900s. The two pioneering child development psychologists were Jean Piaget and Lev Vygotsky. They had similarities and differences between their theories of child development, much like many psychologists. Since then, various psychologists have developed similar theories that agree and disagree with both Piaget and Vygotsky.

Jean Piaget, the Swiss child psychologist, produced the first child development theory called 'the Cognitive Theory', which talked about the nature and growth of human intelligence. In this construct theory put forward by Piaget, he discusses the kind of knowledge children need to acquire and how they acquire it.

According to Piaget, there are four stages of child development, the sensorimotor stage (0–2 years), preoperational stage (2–7 years), concrete operational stage (7–11 years), and formal operational stage (adolescence to adult). In the time before Piaget, psychologists generally believed that children possessed limited thinking skills compared to adults. After observing and working with his children, Piaget theorized that children think very differently to adults, rather than just that they are not as bright as adults. Piaget asserted that children are born genetically equipped with the fundamental reasoning, the building blocks, which they develop over time at their own pace.

The Sociocultural Theory, as put forward by Lev Vygotsky, the Russian child psychologist, however, disagreed with Piaget and claimed that a child's development could be fast-tracked to a certain extent by good scaffolding and with a 'zone of proximal development' (ZPD). This means that when children are young, they are unable to carry out certain tasks and require input from adults to learn new skills and become competent and help themselves as they grow. Vygotsky further asserted that these skills can be enhanced even more with continued adult interaction.

Both Piaget and Vygotsky have valid points and further research in this area shows that both theories work. Children acquire certain skills at a certain age; however, their skills can be enhanced with adult support.

What Are Early Interaction Skills?

You may have read or heard professionals talk about children who require 'early interaction skills' to successfully communicate. Early interaction skills are your child's attention, listening, eye contact, turn-taking, understanding of spoken language, and expressive language (talking). These are the skills that a child needs to begin communicating and have their needs met. As adults, we often forget the importance of these day-to-day interactions and almost take them for granted. I mean, can you explain the right amount of eye contact to make in every situation and why this is the way it is?

It is important to remember that, as parents, you are your child's first teachers. Children love to copy what adults do. As an adult in your child's life, it is your responsibility to be a good interaction and language role model for your child to imitate. Whether this is for the language you use, the way you behave, or even the way you interpret and react to situations. You can't scold your two-year-old for shouting, 'Oh my god' in the supermarket when you said it two minutes earlier.

Children learn these early skills by watching and listening to what is being said. They learn to stay focussed enough to hear, take turns copying your facial expressions, tone of voice, gestures, and words. Children are born with interaction skills. For example, your baby will interact with you using crying and cooing.

For a communication attempt to be successful, we need to be able to attend to what is being said (pay attention), we need to look at the person who is talking (eye contact), listen to and understand the words, then respond appropriately with body language and/or words. When children are learning these skills, they will make mistakes, as they are not yet aware that they need to look at you when you are speaking. They may not be able to attend to what you are saying. They may walk away while you are talking to them. Children learn these skills naturally from the adults in their environment, and continue developing and refining them as they grow. However, there will be children who require extra help to learn these skills. Children who need a little help will learn and adapt within a short time, when these skills are practised through various scenarios. Some children may require further help from a professional as there may be a medical reason for their delay.

There is usually a reason behind any delay. It could be parents are not able to give the quality of attention the child requires because there are other siblings in the house who need more attention. Please don't beat yourself up at this stage. Difficult life situations come about, and we aren't at our best, despite trying our hardest. There could also be a medical reason, learning difficulties, etc. Whatever the reason, the most important thing is that you have picked up this book and are ready to make changes. You can apply the same rules if your child is older and has not yet mastered these skills – just start at the stage they can cope with and then build on the success at each stage.

As parents, we are all guilty of using the television as a babysitter and this is ok up to a point, but if your child is delayed with their developmental skills then you need to rethink this strategy. Television can be good, as it helps children learn lots of vocabulary – sometimes not all good! If your child is anything like mine were and still are, they will be sitting with their mouths slightly open and staring at the screen. This is not interaction. Interaction is a two-way conversation. We will talk about how to use the TV and technology to our advantage later on.

Children need one-to-one social interaction to be able to learn skills like making eye contact with the person who is talking to them, waiting for their turn to speak, understanding simple instructions, and of course to learn to use words or signs to communicate their wants and needs.

As parents, you spend the most time with your child. Therefore, you must support them to build their early skills by modelling and 'scaffolding' their language. The more you practise the early interaction strategies with them, the quicker they will learn the skills and become more confident and competent in their communication abilities.

When you have tried these strategies for two to three months and your child is still not making any progress, or if you feel your child is significantly delayed with their skills by looking at the ages and stages, please consult your medical doctor or specialist to get advice and support.

If you have already made a referral to a speech and language therapy service and are waiting for an initial appointment, please continue to use these strategies and let your therapist know what you have been trying and if you have noticed any progress in your child.

In this book, you are given advice and ideas on how you can use **five minutes** daily to support your child to learn new or enhance and establish current skills, so make every minute count!!

Why Children Need These Skills

How many times have you talked to your partner, maybe asked them a question and you are gobsmacked when they do the complete opposite? Or maybe your parents ask what to buy your children for birthday gifts, but they buy that toy piano you really didn't need! It's normal to wonder if anyone is actually listening! Attention skills are crucial in life, as you need to concentrate on anything you want to do well. We all learn these skills as children and continue to develop them into adulthood. We need to help children to develop these skills, which helps them to become good communicators.

It is important to teach children the skill of making eye contact with the person talking to them. We need eye contact to communicate our feelings or intentions to others. We can show our emotions through our eyes. For example: rolling our eyes when bored when a friend is telling the same story for the 10th time. We show anger, excitement and sadness through our eyes. Eye contact is crucial for successful communication to take place. When someone is talking to you, you look at them. Even if this is your child and you are busy trying to finish other jobs. This shows that you are giving them your full attention, and you are listening to what they are saying. If you do not make eye contact as an adult, you are seen as being rude and disrespectful. Make the wrong amount of eye contact and the situation becomes awkward.

With children, we need to look at it a little differently as they are still learning this skill. If a child does not look at you when you are talking, then they are not attending to what you are saying, and therefore they will not know what you have said and will not carry out the instructions you give them.

In some cultures, it is seen as disrespectful for children to make direct eye contact with adults. Many years ago, in the Western world, some children used to be given a diagnosis of having delayed social communication skills or social communication difficulties, because they would not make eye contact with the professional in clinic.

Travelling around the world has become a norm, as of course has the Internet. Therefore, we have more access to other countries and cultures. This has given us more understanding of how other people communicate, especially interaction rules between adults and children. We can now understand that when a child is reluctant to make eye contact with you in the clinic, it does not necessarily mean that they have social communication difficulties. They might be shy or nervous, or perhaps it is just a sign of their cultural differences.

We need turn-taking skills to be able to communicate with people. Children need this skill to play with their peers, to share a toy or an activity. They need to wait for their turn to speak and answer the questions in the classroom. Children learn this skill early – remember when babies 'coo' and if you 'coo' back, you can have 'a conversation' with your baby just using 'cooing'. We will focus on lots of games and activities that can help develop turn-taking skills.

Ages and Stages of Development

There are stages of how and when early interaction skills develop. Each skill is expected to develop at a certain age. Remember, they are guidelines. By two years old, most toddlers can say around 50 words. If your little one is only up to 45, there is no need to panic.

Some children will develop these skills by watching. However, others will need your help to learn the skills they require.

Babies: They babble, cry to get attention, and turn towards the adult when they speak. They should be able to copy sounds and facial expressions.

Babies develop the following skills between birth and three months:

- Starting to identify the sound of their mother's voice
- Becoming calm and smiling when an adult speaks to them
- Turning their head towards a familiar person's voice and sounds
- Making noises showing pleasure
- Crying differently to show different demands
- Grunting, giggling, whimpering and gurgling

- Starting to coo (repeating the same sounds often) in answer to peoples' voices
- Making sounds that are like vowel sounds – e.g., 'ooh' and 'ah'

Between the ages of three and six months, most babies acquire the following skills:

- Turning their head toward a person who is talking
- Becoming interested in watching the mouth movements of a person who is talking
- Responding to variations in the tone of voice
- Making loud sounds including shrieks
- Vocalizing enthusiasm, pleasure and annoyance
- Crying differently when they are uncomfortable or hungry
- Expressing needs with hand movements
- Babbling to get an adult's attention
- Imitating sounds, inflections and gestures

12 months: The baby begins to understand simple one keyword instructions/routines such as 'Stop', 'No' and 'Sit down'. Babies will continue to copy adults' sounds and react to simple requests from adults. Your baby will start to enjoy clapping games. Repeat sounds and gestures to gain attention (Ages and stages, Child Development Institute, 2004).

Delayed skills: If you have observed that your baby is not as active as described above, please consult your doctor to get advice.

Age two years: Children should be able to point to their body parts when named by an adult – e.g., eyes, nose, hands. Children at this age should be putting together two-word phrases to express themselves or making comments about what is happening around them, e.g., 'Mummy chair', 'Daddy gone'.

Children should be able to follow simple instructions about routines in the home – e.g., 'Pass me the remote, please', 'Let's go out', 'Bath time', 'Bedtime', 'Dinnertime'. They should enjoy listening to short stories/singing rhymes.

They should be able to copy behaviours they see in their environment, e.g., brushing hair, hoovering, dusting, reading books (looking at pictures), asking for more food, or a favourite toy. Self-feeding skills should be developing well by now.

Delayed skills: You should seek help and support if, at this age, your child is not responding when you call them. They are not using lots of single words and at least a few two-word phrases to express their needs. Also, seek advice if your child is not able to understand basic instructions. If you live in a bilingual or multilingual home, don't be worried if this is achieved a little later. They are such amazing little sponges that they are absorbing the languages and speaking often takes a little longer.

Age three years: Children should be able to recognize and name common objects around the home. They should be using two- and three-word phrases to communicate their needs. Their attention levels should be growing and they now should be able to attend to an adult-led activity for a short time.

Delayed skills: Please seek help if your child is not able to understand simple instructions and they are not using short phrases to communicate.

Age five years: Children should be able to talk using short sentences and using complex connective language – e.g., 'We are going to the park because I want to go on the big swings and then we are going to get some food'. They should be able to understand concept words like big/bigger and concept of time like yesterday and tomorrow, first, next, and days of the week, etc.

They should be able to understand positional concepts like first, middle, and last. They should enjoy playing with other children, dress themselves, and be able to answer simple questions.

Delayed skills: Delayed attention and listening skills can have a massive impact on all areas of learning. For example, a four-year-old child may not be able to focus for two to three minutes on any activity, and they may follow their agenda and they do not respond to the adult's instructions. This child is more than likely to have difficulties sharing activities with their siblings or sitting for a meal. They will have trouble staying calm when they are outside in stores, or when they are told that they cannot have a certain food or a toy. They will have problems waiting for their turn to talk or to take turns in a play activity with another child. They will likely become upset and walk away from the activity altogether, preferring to do their own thing.

This child will struggle to listen in nursery/school, as they will not be able to attend to an adult-led task. They may struggle to understand their teacher's instructions. They may also struggle to sit and learn new skills like reading, writing, painting, drawing or even age-appropriate play because they find it difficult to sit and focus for long enough to complete any meaningful activity.

A child described above will require lots of adult support to develop these skills. The child can make progress, but it will only happen with lots of practice over a period of time. Some children learn quickly, and others need a prolonged period of practice. It is recommended that you persevere and continue practising the strategies provided and with time your child will learn these skills with your help. Please see the ages and stages to determine any delay.

In the UK, your child is seen and assessed by a health visitor when they are two years old. You should mention any concerns that you have with them. It may seem to you that two is too young, given that communication skills aren't fully developed until the age of five and upwards. However, early intervention is essential for child development and it doesn't hurt to check at this age. These could be concerns about your child's hearing, understanding, talking, behaviour, feeding and other areas of development. The health visitor will talk to you about your concerns and advise appropriately. You should consult your family doctor for advice if the health visitor is not accessible.

If your concerns are regarding your child's speech and language development, the health visitor can refer your child to a Speech and Language Therapy Service for assessment and advice.

How You Can Help Your Child

If you have referred your child to a speech and language therapist and are waiting for an appointment, then this is the perfect time to use this book. When you attend your speech therapy appointment, let your therapist know what strategies you have been trying out, and whether these have helped your child to develop these skills since their referral.

If you have not referred your child to a speech therapist yet and you want to try these strategies first, then that is fine too. After working on these skills for at least two to three months, if you find that your child has not progressed to reach their age level, then it is time to make a referral.

Attention and listening: Think about this before you start interacting with your child. Do you have your child's full attention? Is your child looking at you? Have they stopped what they were doing and looked at you when you called their name? If you have answered no to any of these questions, then you do not have your child's full attention – therefore, you need to change that before you start talking to them. Timing is key! Just imagine giving your child their favourite colouring book and one minute later asking them to pay attention.

When you are trying to get your child's full attention, first, get rid of all the distractions. For example, switch the TV off, call your child's name, make sure they are looking at you then say 'Sam, give me the book, please', 'It's tidy-up time', etc. As your child grows, their attention levels grow too. However, this is not true for all children. Some children will require more adult support to develop their attention and listening skills. Play lots of games to develop your child's attention and listening skills.

If your child passed the hearing test at birth, and you feel that they react when you talk to them or they answer back when you call them from another room, then that is great. If you feel your child does not answer when you call them or ignores you, they watch the television with high volume, or they look at your mouth when you speak, then talk to your doctor to make sure your child does not have any hearing issues. It is quite common for young children to develop ear infections; these issues can be easily resolved.

Here is one game that helps to develop attention skills:

- Start by getting down to your child's level (face-to-face).
- Say 'Let's play.'
- Offer a choice of two toys.
- Let your child make a choice.
- Start the game (e.g., jigsaw puzzle board).
- You keep all the pieces, and put the puzzle board in front of your child. Hold out two pieces (one in each hand). Name them, and say, 'Which one would you like, car, or truck?'
- Let your child choose and help them place the jigsaw piece in the puzzle board.
- Continue the game until the board is complete. If your child continues to sit, play again, or get another jigsaw puzzle or another game.
- Make sure you praise good sitting and good listening.
- If your child wants to take control of the game, then ask them to be the 'teacher'. Help them to offer you the two choices and name them, then you make the choice and continue the game.
- If, however, your child does not want to play with you, see what they are interested in and you go and sit nearby.
- Get closer if they let you.
- Get another same or similar toy and start to copy their play.

- When they notice you mirroring their game, they will enjoy this parallel play and may continue to play, watching you to see if you are copying them. You are now 'sharing attention'. (Even if it is only for a minute, you can build on this over time.)
- If they move away and tell you not to copy, then stay a little further back and play alone or with another child but make it sound fun. Over time, they will start to pay attention and will want to join you in your game.
- If your child shows no interest in playing at all, don't try to force it, and don't take it personally. Try again in half an hour, or maybe an hour.

Practise active listening when interacting with your child:

There are three levels of active listening: repeating or copying, paraphrasing, and reflecting or mirroring.

'What is the difference between active and reflective listening?' I hear you ask. There is a basic overlap between the two. A person needs to be an active listener to be able to reflect what the speaker is saying.

A reflective listener, on the other hand, is an active listener who does not have to always reflect; they could repeat or paraphrase what has been said.

Here is an example for each of the three levels:

Repeating: Your child says, 'I want a biscuit.' You say, 'Oh, you want a biscuit.'

Paraphrasing: Your child says, 'I want a biscuit.' You say, 'Oh, you're hungry so you want a biscuit.'

Reflecting: Your child says, 'I don't want to play with my sister.' You say, 'Oh, you don't want to play with her because she won't share her toys with you.'

Before you start practising active listening:

- Make sure your child has your full attention.
- Stop what you are doing and make eye contact with your child. This is essential for model behaviour.
- Be face-to-face.
- Reflect or repeat what they are saying to you.
- **Turn-Taking:** Use simple turn-taking tasks, whether specifically or just in your daily routines. You are probably doing this already without even realizing it.
- Sit on the floor, opposite your child. Say to your child, 'Let's play.' You are going to play the game (chosen by your child).
- Start the game – e.g., building a tower with blocks. You keep all the blocks. Offer your child two blocks and name the colours, e.g., red

block/blue block, and let them choose one. Say, 'Oh, you've got red, and I've got blue.'

- Let your child take the first turn.
- Now say, 'It's my turn' and add your block to the tower. If your child tries to grab the block from you, encourage them to wait by saying, 'Please wait, it's my turn, please wait for your turn.' Continue to encourage them to do 'good waiting'.
- Offer two blocks, and let them choose one (say, 'Look, Mummy is doing good waiting!!')
- If your child breaks the tower and becomes upset and leaves the area, continue building the tower and make it sound fun: talk to yourself! E.g. 'Wow, big tower/tall tower/I am going to break the tower.' Ask your child, 'Do you want to help me push/break the tower?' Hopefully, they will re-join you. If they have completely moved away and are not interested, try again tomorrow or later when they are in a better mood!!
- They will over time learn to sit with you and play a lovely turn-taking game.
- In the meantime, you could try other non-games that your child will not even realize they are waiting for a turn – see the last chapter.

Children love to please adults. Your specific praise will help them to learn what the exact skill they are using is 'good' and you are happy with. They will continue to do that over and over to get your attention and praise.

Eye contact: When you are teaching your child about making eye contact, it is important to show them what this looks like. Here are some examples for you to try.

- You are sitting down together on the floor opposite each other to play the 'ready, steady, go' game using a car. You say, 'Ready...' (pause), 'steady...' (pause), and wait for your child to look at you. If they are not looking, then say their name, hold the car next to your face when they look, then say 'Go' and roll the car to them.
- When your child comes up to you and starts talking but they are not looking at you, try not to respond immediately. This is going to feel horrible, but I promise you this will work!
- When they realize that you have not responded, they will repeat themselves.
- If they are still not looking at you, you can say, 'Are you talking to Mummy?'
- You could say something like, 'I am sorry, I did not know you were talking to me, because you

were not looking at me.' 'I could not see your eyes.' 'If you want to talk to me, I need to see your eyes.'

- If your child continues to talk but does not make eye contact, you can move into a position lower than their face, making sure you are in their 'eye line' (so they can just look at you without lifting their head) and say, 'What can Mummy help you with?'

Sometimes children and adults self-talk (talking to yourself) and when they talk while engrossed in their play, they are not asking or expecting you to respond or talk. If you only respond when your child looks at your face, they are asking you to respond. If your child is now in the habit of talking to you without making eye contact, then this strategy will work. Just try it for five minutes each day: sit together, be available, play together if your child wants you to. However, don't respond until your child looks at your face. If they do, then repeat back the last word they say or if they have lots of single-word vocabulary, then you can start adding another word to their single word and repeat it back to them. If they look at your face but don't say anything, then just smile back. Remember, it is ok to be silent, especially in this situation, as you are encouraging eye contact.

If you do this often enough, your child will learn that they need to look at you when they are talking to you or want something from you.

- You need to do the same. When you talk to your child, make sure you have their full attention and especially eye contact. In time, they will learn to generalize this skill and use it with other people.
- Give lots of specific praise when your child starts to look at you when talking, like: 'You did **good looking**; well done.'

Chapter 2

What Is Babble?

'Bababaa... dadididi... mamama...' Babies make these types of sounds when they are about 5 to 10 months old. This phase is extremely crucial as it is the beginning of your baby's language development.

These sounds are not like any language, but this is how your baby begins to communicate with you. Recent studies show that the age your baby starts to babble will determine when they start saying their first words.

How Babies Communicate

Babies are born with the skills that enable them to communicate their needs to their parents. A baby's first communication skill is to cry. These cries become more refined as the baby grows. They will be able to let you know what they need by using different types of crying. As parents, you will very quickly be able to differentiate between your baby's cries. You will be able to work out whether the baby is hungry, has a dirty nappy, is in pain or they just want some attention.

As parents, you will find that there is not always a good reason for a baby to cry. They could just be a little overwhelmed by the noises in their surroundings and crying is the only way they can 'get rid' of that environmental stimulus. Babies and crying are one of Mother Nature's amazing things. Just as your baby is learning, so are you. What sounds like one sound to an outsider can tell a parent a whole different story.

Why Babble Is Important

When you imitate your child's sounds, it tells them that you are interested in what they are doing/saying. This will motivate them to babble again, and you can turn this into a game of copycat! These types of copying games develop your child's ability to take turns, communicate and pay attention to you. It also encourages them to purposefully make sounds to get your attention.

You must be your child's interpreter. If you can work out what your child is telling you when they babble, put this message in your own words and say it back to them. For example, if your child looks at a teddy and says 'Dadada,' you could interpret this by saying, 'Teddy?/You want teddy?' while you point to the teddy. As you begin to interpret your child's messages in this way, you are providing names for the things they are trying to talk to you about. This will build their vocabulary.

Delayed skills: Children with delayed speech sound development or babble are at higher risk for language delay. If your baby is over five months old and still not babbling or turning their head towards you when you talk or make loud noises nearby, please contact your family doctor, first of all, to check if the baby has a hearing problem.

In the UK, babies are given a hearing test soon after birth. Any hearing problems should be picked up at this stage. However, some children will pass this initial hearing test and then may develop hearing problems later.

Ages and Stages of Babble

The baby's first communication with the world is that first cry as soon as they are born. Babies over time learn other sounds like 'cooing' and laughing. Initially, these sounds are unintentional. However, over time and practise with you, these will become intentional.

When you respond to your baby's cooing by cooing back at them, they will coo again, and you can keep going!! When the baby is between 5 to 10 months old, these single sounds then turn into little syllable sounds like 'Da' or 'Di'. This type of babble is called canonical babbling. This can include a string of repeated syllables (e.g., 'Ba ba') or a variety of syllables (e.g., 'Ma di da'). Canonical babbling is an important developmental milestone in a baby's development of language. These are the kind of sounds that the baby will make when they begin to talk. These types of sounds are known as 'jargon'.

Some facts about babbling: Babies use the sounds they hear in their environment. The consonant sounds that babies use in their babble are mostly the consonant sounds that will eventually be in their first words.

Babies who have multiple languages spoken in their environment will babble just as much as babies who have only one language.

How You Can Help Your Baby

Some babbling is intentional, and you will be able to tell that your baby is trying to tell you something. Sometimes it is not clear if the babbling has a message. It can be difficult for parents to decipher how, when and if to respond when your child is having fun with different sounds.

Wait for your child to start their babble. Before children start talking properly, it is quite easy to fill in the gaps with your own words. However, if you say nothing and just wait for your child to begin, this will encourage them to start making sounds when they are ready.

Watch your child carefully when they babble. It will tell you if their babble is meant to send you a message or not. If you see your child looking at or pointing to an object while they babble, or trying to get your attention, their babble is likely to be purposeful and they are trying to send you a specific message.

When you see your baby babbling while they are engrossed in play and they are not trying to get your attention, this means that they are just having fun playing around with different sounds and just practising their new skills.

Chapter 3

What Is Understanding of Language?

Understanding of language or receptive language is the capacity to learn words and grammar. It involves getting information and knowledge from your routines, like 'I have my coat on, now I can go out'. We also learn by watching what others are doing. For example, Daddy holding his keys means that we are going out in the car. We learn that words like 'ball' means a round bouncy object that we can play with. We also learn about grammar (e.g., regular plurals: cat/cats, regular past tense: fetch/fetched) and written information (e.g., signs in the environment like 'No Ball Games' and written stories).

Understanding of language includes being able to follow instructions, understand concepts, grammatical elements, sentence structure, questions, and understanding stories and written text.

Why Understanding of Language Is Important

Understanding language is necessary to communicate successfully. Children who have problems with their understanding will find following instructions difficult at home and in school and may not be able to respond appropriately to questions and requests.

In the school setting, problems in understanding spoken language will lead to attention and listening difficulties and/or behavioural concerns. Most activities need a good understanding of language. Otherwise, it will be difficult for a child to access the school curriculum or get involved in the activities and tasks required in school.

Observe your child and see if you can answer the following questions:

- Is your child able to follow simple instructions supported with clues? For example, when you tell them to get you something you may also be giving them a clue by looking and pointing at the item.
- Is your child able to follow instructions without clues?

- Is your child able to identify one item out of four that are placed in front of them without clues?
- Is your child able to carry out instructions containing action words? For example, 'Make the doll jump', 'Make the teddy sleep'.
- Look at the Ages and Stages of Development section and see if your child's understanding is at the level it should be.

Ages and Stages of Development

We will look at more specific speech and language development below. The following is a quick overview.

1–2 years: Children begin to understand simple one-keyword instructions like 'Stop' and 'No'. They should also understand instructions like 'Where is the **cup**?' (from a choice of two items, maybe a cup and a spoon).

2–3 years: Children should be able to understand instructions containing two key words like: 'Go to the **bedroom** and bring your **coat**' (key words are 'bedroom' and 'coat').

3–4 years: Children can understand instructions containing three key words like: 'Point to the **car,**

truck, and the **motorbike**' (from a choice of at least five different types of vehicles).

4–5 years: Children at this age should be understanding instructions containing four key words. For example, 'Give the **big red car** to **teddy**' (from a choice of big and little red cars, big and little cars of another colour and teddy and a dolly).

For instruction to count as key words, you must have an option to choose from when the instruction is given. Your child can then pick up the items you have requested if they have understood the instruction. If there are no other choices, then it does not count as a keyword because your child can just pick up the item that is there, without having to understand your words.

What Is Expressive Language?

Expressive language is your child's ability to use language to express themself. Your child uses words/signs every time they want to have their needs met, or to express their feelings and ideas to other people by using words and sentences.

If your child is unable to express themselves as expected for their age, these types of difficulties with vocabulary will fall into the category of delayed expressive language.

Why Expressive Language Is Important

Expressive language is important as it helps us express our needs, wants, emotions and ideas. It helps us make an argument for and against an idea. Children need to develop their use of this language to engage in successful interactions with others. They also need the language to develop their writing skills when in school.

If your child is not able to communicate with you using words or signs, they will become frustrated because you are not able to meet their needs in the exact way that they want. It is extremely important for children to learn to use single words or signs between the age of 12–18 months. As they grow older, these single words and signs will become short phrases.

If the delay is significant, your speech and language therapist may suggest using the Core Vocabulary Approach to help your child learn and expand their vocabulary. They will initially ask you to think of at least 50 words that your family consistently uses when communicating with each other. Please see examples below, of what core vocabulary may include.

The games suggested in this book are useful in teaching vocabulary. Help your child to learn the basic vocabulary in their environment, even before they can talk. Your child needs to hear the words lots and lots of times first before attempting to say them. It can feel like you are talking to yourself, but I promise you have an attentive audience, albeit rather little.

Delayed skills: Look at the ages and stages to find out what is expected of your child at their age. If you feel that your child's skills are delayed, then you now have the tools to help them. When you have tried these strategies for two to three months and your child is still not making any progress, please consult your medical doctor or specialist to get advice and support. If you have already made a referral to a Speech and Language Therapy Service and are waiting for an initial appointment, please continue to use these strategies and let your therapist know what strategies you have been trying and if you have noticed any progress.

Core Vocabulary: The words which are required and are frequently used by us to verbally communicate (express ourselves) are called our core vocabulary. The most notable features of a core vocabulary are that it is quite small in number and can be used across all environments of the person. According to research, 85% of what we say is communicated with only 200 basic words.

Core vocabulary includes the following types of words that help the child to communicate their needs and wants. When they have learned these words, they can combine them to make short phrases. These words can apply across all settings.

- Pronouns (I, he, she, mine)
- Verbs (play, stop, look, drink, eat, is)
- Describing words, (big, little, nice, red, blue)
- Prepositional words (in, on, under, near)
- A few frequently used noun words will be included in the core vocabulary (names/titles of family members e.g., Mum/Dad, foods, house, home, bathroom, bedroom)

Ages and Stages of Development – Word Levels

When we look at word level development, we concentrate on the average number of words a child can say and then how they start stringing these words together to form short sentences and understand. As the months pass by, you will also notice their vocabulary bank starts to include different parts of speech.

12 to 18 months: Your child should have at least 20 single words that they understand. These are mostly nouns/names of things. You will hear lots of repetitions at this stage. They will start putting two words together to make a phrase.

2 years: Your child should have between 150 to 300 single words. These will include names of family members, names of things they encounter in their environment daily – e.g., food, drinks, toys, television programs, and the words they will hear you and their siblings saying. Some of these words may not be 'good' words, so be careful what you say in front of them!! They are little parrots and will repeat anything without understanding the meaning.

3 years old: They should have about 1,000 single words. They will now be using more action words (verbs) – e.g., running, sitting, eating, etc.

They will be able to use some past tenses when talking about something that has happened in the recent past. They will have regular plurals, e.g., book/books, apple/apples, shoe/shoes. The child should now be using three-word phrases – e.g., 'my red pen', and be able to answer simple questions like 'What is your name?' 'Are you a boy or a girl?' 'How old are you?'

Most children's speech should be clear at this age. However, there will be a small percentage of children who will have unclear speech and only you as parents can understand them.

4 years: Children will be able to use prepositional words like 'in', 'on', and 'under'. They will be able to correctly identify colours and numbers up to 10.

5 years: Your child should be able to count to 10 if not more. Children's speech at this age should be clear, where everyone can understand what they are saying, and they should be using sentences with correct grammar.

What Are Blank Levels of Questioning?

Blank Levels of Questioning is a method used to develop verbal reasoning in children. It was developed by Blank, Rose, and Berlin in 1978. The three spent time watching teachers in a classroom. They found that questions could be categorized into four levels, starting with the basic and leading up to questions that require problem-solving skills and abstract answers. There are four levels:

- **Level 1:** the ability to name things
- **Level 2:** the ability to describe things and answer simple questions
- **Level 3:** the ability to talk about stories and different events
- **Level 4:** the ability to solve problems and answer more detailed questions as well as 'why' questions

It's estimated that 60% of three-year-olds can understand levels 1 and 2. Approximately 65% of five-year-olds can understand levels 3 and 4. Let's take a little look at each in more detail so that later, you can incorporate this into your games.

Level 1

At this level, we are working towards children matching immediate perception to language. There is a combination of looking and listening. You can ask your child to point to different objects, pick them up or pass them to you. They will understand what a matching object is and find you one. They will start to answer the question 'What is this?'.

Level 2

During level 2, children will still have the answer to your questions in front of them but they will have to think and search for it. There are more language concepts at this level. So, rather than asking them to pass you an object, you will ask them to pass you the big or small object. You can ask your child to explain what is happening in different situations or finish sentences like 'We eat our cereal with a...'. Question words will include 'who', 'what', and 'where'.

Level 3

Bear in mind that at this level, children will already have an understanding of language so that they can find a clue and then create their own answer. They will be able to generalise, group information, and follow a set of instructions. They can find links with other objects, so you might be able to ask them about another type of transport that has four wheels instead of two. They will have developed storytelling skills and will be able to arrange pictures into a sequence and then tell you a story about the pictures. You can ask them what will happen next or about how certain characters in the story feel. At this level, children will be able to tell you what some words mean.

Level 4

This is where reasoning really kicks in. They start to develop the ability to solve problems by thinking about the different relationships between objects. At this point, they can identify the cause of a problem and find a solution. They will begin to see things from other people's points of view and understand what they would do to solve a problem. When there is no solution, they will be able to explain why. On that note, all 'why' questions fall into this level. Furthermore, children might be able to explain the logic behind compound words, such as 'Why is it called a pencil case?'.

The levels are not always quite as clear cut as this. You may notice your child grasping parts of level 2 before they have mastered all of level 1. To help children move through the stages, you can:

- Give your child time to process the question and respond.
- Make sure your child is focused on the activity.
- Repeat the question, rephrase it, or simplify it.
- Give sound cues, like the first sound of the answer.
- Draw your child's attention to the answer by pointing to clues.
- Show the answer by demonstrating what would happen rather than explaining.
- Remind children of previous experiences that will help them find the answer.

How You Can Help Your Child

Children are born with basic interaction skills. For example, your baby will interact with you by using crying and cooing. As your child continues to grow physically, it is also important to help them continue developing their communication skills. The skills they learn and use to communicate in the first five years are called the 'early interaction skills'.

Examples of early interaction skills include waving, shrugging shoulders, and a wide range of facial expressions to express emotions such as surprise.

For a communication attempt to be successful, we need to be able to pay attention to what is being said. We need to look at the person who is talking, listen and understand what they are saying and then respond appropriately.

We as adults know that to ask a question, respond to a question or a comment and make a request, we need these skills. Children need to be taught these skills so that they can become competent communicators. One of the most natural and effective ways is to teach through play.

Most children will learn these skills from the adults in their environment. However, some children will require extra help. Children who need a little extra help will learn and adapt within a short time but there will be children who may need further help from a professional.

Children need one-to-one interaction or talking to someone face-to-face, where they can practise the skills, we want them to learn skills like attention, listening, turn-taking, and learning how to ask for what they want and respond to simple requests.

- As soon as your child can understand basic instructions like 'Stop' and 'No', start to teach them basic vocabulary by naming things that they encounter.
- Use single key words. Repeat the word two or three times in different ways to instil the meaning, while showing them the item you are naming. For example, if your child is playing with a car, you can say 'Car', 'Red car', 'Big car'.
- For children not using words yet, you can use symbolic noises that things make, as well as the words. For example, beep for a car, woof for a dog, meow for a cat, etc.
- Comment on the play. Try not to ask too many questions as your child does not have the vocabulary to answer your questions. For example, when you see your child playing with

his car, instead of saying 'What are you doing?' say, 'You are playing with your car?'

- You can ask questions that only require a yes/no answer, or when a child must make a choice and say one word, like, 'Do you want apple or orange?' or 'Do you want some milk?' That being said, don't ask a yes/no question if you are hoping for a certain outcome. While this isn't related to speech and language development, it does make life easier. At bedtime, you wouldn't ask 'Do you want to go to bed?' – what will you do if they say no?!

- When we speak to young children who are still developing their early skills, we should be using verbal and non-verbal clues to help them understand our questions, instructions and requests.

- This is especially important when you are teaching them the new vocabulary. For example, pointing to things, e.g., 'Give me the remote, please.' Now your child knows what the remote is and what they can call it.

- Show them their coat and say, 'Let's put your coat on and go out.' Now your child will know the name for a 'coat' and will learn that they need a coat when going out with you.

- Another strategy we suggest you use is 'giving options' for everything. For example, if your child points to the fridge and makes a sound, you take them to the fridge and see what they point to. If they point to a carton of juice, then pick up the juice and something you know they will not want, like broccoli. Hold both items in each hand, out of reach so they cannot just grab what they want, and ask 'Do you want juice or broccoli?' If your child can say 'Juice' then great, give them the juice and say, 'Here is your juice; mmm, **cold juice.**' Now you have added language to their single word by adding one of your own. Next time your child will try and say 'Juice' if you say it to them often enough. However, if your child does not know the word for juice and usually points to what they want, then accept their pointing as 'request' and say, 'Oh, you want juice?' 'Here is your juice', 'Mmm, juice'. Make sure you emphasize the word 'juice' as you are teaching this word. Your child has now heard you say the word 'juice', and they understand what it is called but are not able to say the word yet. Continue to do this every time they ask for juice. Do this for everything where possible.

- Research shows that a child needs to hear the same word at least 200 times before they can say it. So be patient and PERSEVERE!! You will start to notice a difference and probably sooner than you had imagined.

- Try making comments using simple one or two words to develop understanding and basic vocabulary. For example, when you are making a tower using blocks, instead of saying, 'Is that a big tower?' say, 'Wow, big tower', or 'Little tower', or 'Wobbly tower'. Your child will understand the words like 'big' and 'little' and in time they will start to generalize the use of these words in other situations.

Here is an example of how you could check whether your four-to-five-year-old child can understand instructions containing four key words. You can use different colours or items if you do not have these items or colour suggested here, BUT you must give your child two options for each item.

- Two red cars, one big and one small
- Two blue cars, one big and one small
- One teddy
- One doll
- Give the instruction, 'Give the **little blue car** to **teddy**'. If they can do it then great. Give another instruction. If not, show them what you wanted them to do. Give the same instruction again, and praise if they get it right. Continue to give instructions at this level using

different items/scenarios until your child is getting it right 100% of the time.

- You could also try the four-key word instruction as: 'Put the **apple** and **banana** and the **strawberry** in the **basket**.' You can have options of other fruits besides the ones mentioned here and another option besides the basket, to see if your child can identify the apple, banana and strawberry and put them in the basket as you have asked.

- If not, then try three key word instructions like: 'Put the **apple** and the **banana** in the **basket**.' If they are at an age where they should be understanding four key words, then practise using daily activities and modelling the four key word instruction tasks yourself, then ask your child to practise.

- Praise their effort even if they get the answer wrong. Show them the right answer. For example, if your three-to-four-year-old is not able to carry out three key word instructions, practise two key word instructions with them for a few weeks and then try again.

- Remember to say the instruction. If your child is unsure, carry out the instructions, then ask them to copy what you did. When they become confident at carrying out that instruction, try a different one at the same level: 'Pass me three bricks' (from an option of six, seven or more bricks) or 'Can you give me one blue brick and two red bricks?'

- When you have done lots of practice to develop your child's understanding at a certain level, try giving an instruction at that level. If they are now confident and can carry out your instructions in a variety of ways, then move to the next level.

Helping Your Child to Communicate – Clarity of Speech

It always makes me laugh when a toddler or young child is jabbering on and you think you understand what they are saying. When you pass them the red sheep, Mum or Dad says, 'No, he said beep, he wants the car.' I haven't met a single parent who hasn't developed the amazing ability to cipher their child's language. This is still just a developmental stage and they need to be able to correctly identify objects and pronounce them well so that they are understood by other key people in their lives. Here is how we can work on clarity of speech.

- Decrease pressure on speech and do not correct your child.
- Use positive approach/help to build confidence. Encourage your child to give you clues for example gestures/signs showing you what they want, to support their speech.
- Ask yes/no questions or give forced alternatives to help understanding of responses.
- Use a home link or communication book to send to the nursery to find out information and help you understand when your child is retelling you an event that happened in a school and vice versa.
- Repeat back what you think you have understood when your child is talking to check for meaning.

Discrimination/Listening Activities

These activities can help children to focus on you when you are speaking. Therefore, they will develop listening skills and discriminate between sounds.

- 'Ready, steady, go' games
- Sound location (hide a noisemaker and encourage your child to find it)
- Musical bumps/statues

- Musical instruments – listening and finding the matching instrument, copying a rhythm or sequence of sounds. Sound lottos (environmental/symbolic noises)

Rhythm and rhyme:

- Syllable and rhyme awareness normally begins to develop when a child is three/four years old
- Activities to develop these skills will help your child with speech sound difficulties
- Rhythm and syllables
- Copying clapping/drumming patterns
- Clapping syllables in names
- Clapping syllables of familiar things e.g., 'cat' vs 'caterpillar'

Rhyme:

- Rhyme is a good way to develop a child's storage of sounds/words, e.g., 'key' and 'tea'
- Nursery rhymes
- Discriminating between rhyming words. Give your child two words and ask if they rhyme. For example, 'cat' and 'bed'.
- Generating rhymes. Find rhyming pair words together. You could say 'Bake' and they say 'Cake'.

- Identifying rhyming words e.g., 'tap' and 'cap' by themselves.
- Helping production of sounds – repeating mispronounced rhyming words. You can help your child produce the sound correctly by modelling the sound first but this depends on the age of your child.

During everyday conversations, model the right way to say the words for your child, but remember not to correct. Repeat the word correctly but telling them that's not the way to say a word can knock their confidence and prevent them from trying again.

During structured activities, remember the sequence of development (single sound, sound in a word, sound in a short phrase and sound in a sentence). If your child can say the sound on its own – try modelling it back at the beginning of the word with a gap, e.g., 't-a-p', 'c-a-p', 'r-e-d', 'b-e-d'.

Give your child as many clues as you can:

- Encourage them to look at your mouth.
- Look in a mirror together, and say different sounds and short words.
- Talk about how and where the sound is made in your mouth.

Now that your little one is starting to create words, the ability to understand different cries develops into an ability to understand words that others can't decipher. There are so many words that can be misinterpreted, from 'tree' to 'three' and 'sheep' to 'ship'. It's early days, so it's normal that the clarity of speech is another area that will develop. Naturally, you will want to help your child with the clarity of their words, but you can also enjoy this very special connection you have, being able to understand them.

If your child's speech is unclear or you have noticed that you are the only one who can decipher what your child is saying, you need to teach them to produce certain sounds correctly. You can do this by modelling the correct pronunciation of the word when your child pronounces the word using an incorrect sound, or misses the sound out completely. Here are some tips to start working to help your child to have more fluent and clear speech when they talk.

- When your child wants you to give them a 'bo', you might know they mean 'ball', as they might be pointing to a ball or you are now aware that this is how they say the word 'ball'.
- To help your child to learn the word 'ball', give them the ball when they ask, and say the word 'ball': 'Here is your ball', 'Let's play with the ball', (emphasize the ending of the word).

Practise saying other short words that end in the /l/ sound. For example, 'Let's sit on the **wall**', 'Daddy is **tall**', 'Let's **call** mummy', 'Let's play with the **doll**', 'Do not **fall**', 'You **roll** the dice'. Do this for whichever sound they are struggling with.

- You get face-to-face with your child, so down on their level. Hand them the item and say the word e.g., 'Ball, here is your ball'. Again, emphasize the end of the word.

- If your child says or is omitting the initial sound of the word – for example, they might say 'tat' instead of 'cat' or 'sots' instead of 'socks'.

- Being face-to-face helps as your child can see how you are saying the word. However, do not tell your child, 'now you say the word'. They can't be made to feel like they need to perform for you.

- At this point, you just need to model the correct word pronunciations for your child to hear.

- Sometimes children need to hear the words lots and lots of times before they can say them.

- If your child is struggling with a sound, for example, /k/ vs /c/. They might be using a /t/ in its place or they might miss this sound from words altogether.

- Use games and everyday routines to target this word.
- Use the 'I Spy' game to find all the words beginning with /c/ or /k/.
- When out in the stores, find all the things beginning with this sound.
- You say the word a couple of times, show the item to your child and say the name, e.g., 'carrots', 'cake', 'kite', 'kettle'; emphasize the initial sound.
- Having said that, if your child is five and he/she makes lots of errors with their speech sounds, then it is time to get them assessed and get advice.

It is important that you do not ask your child, 'Now, *you* say...') This is to stop your child feeling incapable because if they can't say the correct sound, they will feel they have failed and won't want to engage with you when you play speech sound games. We want to give positive feedback and praise your child's efforts.

Your child may have developed glue ear and may need some intervention from the audiology department. The middle part of the ear canal, which should be empty, gets filled with water. It can cause temporary hearing loss, and this will affect their ability to hear the clarity of your pronunciation.

Focus on what your child is saying, NOT how they are saying it.

One final thought I wanted to mention was not to treat your children as if they are stupid. There is no need to overly emphasise parts of a word or slow down your speech to the point where it doesn't sound natural. That's not how we speak in the real world, so it's not the model language we wish them to learn. It's more likely to be other family members who do this rather than you, but it's good to keep an eye out for it.

Chapter 4

Why Play Skills Are Important

Play is important for developing children's language skills. Look at the following reasons why it is important for children to engage in play:

Play is the basis for literacy development. Children learn and practise their words through play. They learn new vocabulary and extend their pretend play skills.

Play is learning. Children's learning develops through play. There are many different forms of play. For example, playing peek-a-boo games with your baby, to running around in the garden with your three-year-olds.

Play helps adults to interact with their children. As adults in your child's life, you must provide opportunities for your child to experience play.

While playing, adult/child interaction provides a chance for children to listen to the correct speech sounds.

Through play, children learn to be spontaneous. As adults, we believe that toys should be played in a proper way. However, a child might use the basket in which you store their toys in as a hat and walk around. Let them do this; they are using their imagination! Mine used to love wearing the colander as a hat and it cracked me up!!

Play provides children with choice. It is always good to have a choice of things to do and play is no different.

Children need space. Children need space to develop their physical skills and test out what they are capable of.

As an adult, learn how to play again. Refresh your play skills by teaching your child to play using everyday routines in the home. We get so wrapped up in our serious adult lives that we forget how much fun playing can be. Unleash your creativity with playdough!

Adults read their child's body language during play. The more you practise play with your child, the better you will become at knowing when you should join in your child's play.

Adults learn to be patient and understand their children through play. When you play with your child, remember not to take over the play activity and tell them how to play with the toy. It is important to 'follow your child's lead'. Let your child be the leader and you follow their play. If you do this, it is more likely your child will stay with the play activity for a longer period.

Play together and have fun. When children have age-appropriate play skills, they will be able to build better social relationships with their peers.

Ages and Stages to Play

Solitary play: Up to two years of age, children usually play alone, preferring their own toys. Children at this age, usually do not like to interact with other children their age. You should encourage your child to play alone, and this will help them to develop their skills for working independently.

Delayed skills: Give your child an age-appropriate toy. For example, children at this age will enjoy cause-and-effect toys where they press a button and the music plays, etc. If your child is not familiar with the toy, sit with them to demonstrate how to play with it. When your child has become familiar with a toy, do they know how to play with it? Are they showing any interest in any of the toys? Have you tried different types of activities and they are still not showing any interest? Would they rather stay in one place and not interact with their environment? If so, then this would be a time to talk to your doctor.

Parallel play: From two-and-a-half to three, children will continue to enjoy playing by themselves. However, at this age, they start to play beside other children and may use some of the same toys.

Delayed skills: Is your child interested in playing next to other children? If not, encourage them to play next to you at home first. Take them to playgroups so they can see how other children play. Once they are comfortable being around other children, encourage them to play near the other children in the playgroup or the nursery. You can sit with them and model how to play near other children but not join in their play.

Associative play: Three to four-and-a-half years: children will start to play with other children. They will be able to share play materials. However, they will usually follow their own agenda or type of play.

Delayed skills: Children who are used to playing alone at home and who do not like sharing their toys with their siblings will struggle at this stage when they start nursery. However, adults can help them with this skill by practising play in a small group using one toy to share, where children are having to wait to take a turn, therefore learning that they need to share and that it is fun to play together!

If your child is struggling in this area, then you should spend time working on this and seek professional advice, as if this area is delayed, then it is likely that other areas of development will be delayed too.

Cooperative play: Four to five-and-a-half is the most important level of social playing is where children will play together in a group and they will all be contributing to accomplishing a shared purpose. This kind of play requires discussion between children. This occurs when children develop 'characters' in the game and/or take turns giving ideas about the plan.

Delayed skills: If your child is not at a stage where they should be, then please help and support them to get to that stage and beyond by using the strategies suggested below. Also, contact your local Speech and Language Therapy Service for an assessment and further advice, if you are worried that your child is not making progress in this area.

How You Can Help Your Child

You can learn so much by observing your child, see what they are interested in or like doing more than anything else. Do they like watching videos on the iPad, or do they just enjoy physical games and not sitting and completing jigsaw puzzles or sharing toys with their siblings and you?

Get a similar toy to what they are watching on the iPad. For example, if they like watching 'Yakka-dee' (a little girl who loves to talk and teach other children how to say particular words in each episode). Find a toy related to this character, like a jigsaw puzzle or a book. Try and engage your child with this toy, hopefully getting them off the iPad. When they are happy to do that, then move them on to another jigsaw puzzle, to other toys they might pick up at the stores. The aim is to get your child to engage with toys and not just sit there staring at a screen.

If they enjoy physical games ONLY, then instead of running around aimlessly, involve your child to design an outdoor game that you can both do together (practise turn-taking, attention and listening, without them realizing they are doing it!). If you have space in your garden, use chalk to draw a game where they must do different things along the way from start to

- Arrive a little early to help your child settle in the clinic waiting room environment.
- Prepare your child for the appointment. You could say something like 'We are going to see (name of the therapist) and you will get toys to play with and talk to him/her.'
- Some children become anxious and believe that they will be getting an injection, as they may be going to the same health centre where they normally see their doctor for their immunisations.
- Your therapist will come to the waiting room to collect you.
- The therapist will take your child's developmental history.
- They will ask you questions about your child's developmental milestones, such as when your child starts to sit independently. When did they start walking? When did they say their first words? Are there any concerns regarding your child's hearing?
- These questions are asked to establish if your child's skills are developing according to their age or are there other areas of delay besides what they have been referred for.
- You will have an opportunity to discuss your concerns. For example, if you have referred your four-year-old child for not talking in

finish. See the example in the games chapter for outdoor games.

REMEMBER – Do a minimum of five minutes daily but if you have more time or if your child is happy to continue playing, then keep playing!!

Chapter 5

How to Refer Your Child
Speech and Language The
Service

If you live in the United Kingdom, you car
your local Speech and Language Therapy S
look at their referral criteria and how to re

If you are outside of the UK or you are un
process, talk to your family doctor or y
health visitor. If your child has started
their teacher feels that they have a significa
one or more areas of their learning, eith
directly refer or give your consent to y
teacher to refer your child for an assessm
live outside the UK, please search for S
Language Therapy Service, and follow the

What to Expect From Your
Appointment

- You will be given a specific appoint

sentences, the therapist will want to know about your child's understanding of spoken language: How many words can they say? Are they putting any words together to ask you for what they want? What other means is your child using to communicate with you? For example, are they using gestures, signs or are they just taking you to what they want and then just pointing?

- It is important to prepare a little beforehand if possible but do not worry or be anxious as the therapist is there to help and support you.

- The initial assessment can be quite daunting for parents because there are a lot of questions. It will really help if you write down all of the things you want to discuss. All too often, people walk out of a meeting and appointment and think about what they wish they had said. Use the questions as a guideline and make notes of anything else you are worried about.

- After the case history is completed, the therapist may ask you to play with your child while they observe.

- If your child is confident enough and is happy to sit with the therapist, then they will attempt to assess the area of concern through play.

- After talking to you, observing your child, and assessment of early skills, the therapist may book another appointment with you to come back for further assessment. If your child is in school, they will talk to their teacher to get their perspective on your child's difficulties.

- After assessing your child and making a diagnosis based on the results of the assessment and their observations of your child, the Speech and Language Therapist will set targets for your child to work on and make recommendations from evidence-based research. For example, if after assessment, your child's understanding of language is deemed to be at level 2, but they are old enough where they should be able to understand level 4 language (meaning their understanding of language is delayed) then the therapist will set targets for level 3 language as you need to work on the next level rather than going straight to level 4 – because your child needs to learn and practise language at level 3 first.

- The next step might be that your child needs to attend group therapy – for this, you will be invited to attend a group with other parents and children with similar needs.

- Or you may be offered a parent workshop where only parents are invited and a presentation is made by a speech and language therapist (it probably will not be the same therapist). You will be given resources to use at home to help your child and follow the advice given.

- You will be given advice and strategies will be demonstrated and resources/advice sheets/leaflets given to you to use at home.
- A report will be written to explain what happened in the initial appointment and it can be shared – with your consent, of course – with your child's school, family doctor and any other relevant professionals involved.
- I hope this is helpful!

It's time to take a little break! Why don't you go make a cup of tea and then take a few minutes to tell Amazon how you have found this book, informative, interesting, useful etc.

Link below for quick access– thank you so much in advance for your review!

https://www.amazon.com/Speech-Therapy-Year-Olds-Communication-Understanding/dp/B08T4MLM3N/ref

Chapter 6

73 Games to Develop Speech, Language and Play Skills Using Five Minutes a Day!

We aren't reinventing the wheel here. A lot of the games on the list you are probably already playing. What's important now is that you are more aware of speech and language development and you can incorporate techniques into the games. We aren't making new games or going out to buy new toys It's about using what you have at hand to make a difference.

Here is a list of ideas and games you can use to help your child develop their early interaction skills.

BEFORE YOU START!!!

If you are going to practise the early interaction skills through play at home, then please make sure the following things are in place:

- Choose a time when you can give your 100% attention to the activity for at least five minutes (you can continue if your child is enjoying the time with you and wants to keep playing).

- Make sure you eliminate all distractions. Switch the television off.
- Switch your mobile phone off, put it on 'silent' or better yet, leave it in another room.
- If you have other children in the house, try these activities when the other children are occupied and are unlikely to disturb your time with this child.
- Choose a quiet area of the house.
- Offer your child a choice of two toys (they should be toys where you can practise the skill you are targeting).
- REMEMBER: normally, you should follow your child's lead when playing together. However, when you are targeting certain skills, then you will need to take the lead.
- Tell your child, 'It's our **five minutes playtime**!!' Sometimes, it may only be a few minutes and other times it will be more. Just make sure you can dedicate a minimum of five minutes to the activity.
- If you do this every day or a few times a day, your child will anticipate this special time with you and will look forward to having you all to themselves.

- Try and simplify it, or step-up to make it more difficult. For example, if you are playing a dress-up game and you are working on turn-taking skills, then to make it difficult, ask your child to 'be the teacher' and tell you which item of clothing to put on next: e.g., sweater, dress, shoes. If your child does not know the names of most of the items you have chosen, then first teach them the names. If they are still struggling, you can name all the items. For example, 'Jack put on shoes', 'Mummy put on a hat', etc.
- Simplify your language to match your child's language. If your child is only able to use single words, then it is recommended that you use single key words to comment on the game. If your child uses lots of single words, then you can start adding language to their utterances. For example, your child says 'Car', you say 'Yes, it's a car, it's a red car'.
- You can practise all skills discussed in this book using the ideas given below.
- Attention/listening – make sure you have your child's attention before talking to them.
- Discover your child's motivators (what they enjoy doing most). Incorporate the teaching into their preferred activity.

- Give your child time to complete their own choice of activity. You can sit nearby and join in if they want you to. Move to how can you help.
- Understanding – make sure you name the things you are playing with; e.g., colours/dolly/car/blocks/ball/book.
- Talking – talk with a slow speech rate (not robotic!) and use clear single words, making sure your child is looking at you. They may attempt to say the words and phrases you are saying.
- Use lots of positive praise for their efforts and attention and turn-taking skills. Use phrases such as 'good listening', 'good waiting', 'good looking', 'good turn-taking', 'good sharing' and 'good sitting' to encourage these actions.
- The most important thing is to have FUN!

Below are ideas for different games you can play. These games are interchangeable, and any game can be used with any age child. Just remember to step-down if the game is too difficult or step-up if the game is too easy.

1. Blowing bubbles. Blow bubbles, then wait for your child to indicate that they want more. They could do this by tapping you on your arm, making eye contact with you, pointing to the

bottle of bubble solution, or by saying the words, 'More bubbles'.

2. Read different types of books, get your child to turn pages, learn new vocabulary. Ask 'who' questions ('Who is playing?', 'Who is sleeping?').

3. Eye contact – hold the toy next to your face to encourage your child to look at the toy and therefore, they will make eye contact with you.

4. Turn-taking – encourage your child to take a turn with you. Give lots of praise (turning pages in a book, pointing to pictures, rolling a car/ball to you). Then move on to games.

5. Making symbolic noises for animals (cat, dog, lion) or vehicles (aeroplane, car) depending on the age and the ability of your child.

6. Taking a turn in front of a mirror to make funny faces (stick your tongue out/try to touch your nose with the tip of your tongue).

7. Pretend games: talking to Grandma on the telephone. Playing shops or kitchens. Having a pretend teddy bear or superhero picnic.

8. Build something with Lego bricks. Say 'You add one piece, then Mummy's turn'. Encourage them to wait for their turn. (Build a house/car/a wall.)

9. Play with cause-and-effect toys, taking turns to press a button/lever or musical pop-up toys.

10. Play with a jigsaw puzzle. You keep all the pieces, and offer a choice of two when it is your child's turn, naming the pieces, this will help with developing vocabulary.

11. Play the 'ready steady go' game, using a car or a ball (say 'Ready... steady...' and if your child doesn't say 'Go' then you say 'Go').

12. Exploring the home environment will help your child to learn new vocabulary. Let us find something red/green/big/little/noisy/soft etc.

13. Build a tower with some blocks. Make sure you tell your child to wait for their turn. Hold out two different colour blocks and say, 'Do you want blue or red?' When they choose one, praise them for making a choice. When they wait for their turn say, 'Good waiting.' You could also give them a thumbs-up.

14. Play with a teddy or doll, wash, feed, brush its hair, etc.

15. Press a button to take a turn with an online game on the iPad. For slightly older children, you can play vocabulary memory games, taking turns to match pairs on the iPad.

16. Looking at a book with different textures on each page, learning new words like: 'soft', 'hard', 'smooth', 'rough', 'squishy', 'fluffy', 'bumpy' etc.

17. Use a straw to blow bubbles in the water – this will help with developing /f/ and /s/ speech sounds.

18. Naming game – point to your face and say 'Nose.' Ask your child to point to their nose. If they know their features, tell them to be the teacher and choose the next feature you can both point to (eyes/ears/mouth/teeth/hair, etc).

19. Take turns to throw a bean bag/teddy into a basket (make teddy jump into the basket) – make it fun!

20. Encourage your child to engage in their preferred activity – e.g., playing with dinosaurs in the sand tray, colouring sheets, looking at pictures in the reading books. (You be the commentator and supply the vocabulary.)

21. Colour a picture together: 'Your turn to colour, now my turn' (both of you colouring a little bit of the picture at a time).

22. Pour water into a container using cups at bath time. 'My turn, now your turn.' (Try holding the cup high or low when pouring water.)

23. Build a sandcastle together when on the beach or have wet sand at home.

24. Create a shaving foam tray. You can hide toys in the foam and name them together as you

find them. Older children can use their finger to trace letters in the shaving foam.

25. Play dress-up – pretend to be a superhero; e.g., Spider-Man.

26. Sing nursery rhymes then stop halfway. See if your child was paying attention and continues the song (use words/signs and actions). Make a mistake singing the rhyme. If your child is paying attention, will they correct you. If not, you say 'Oops, I think I made a mistake, can you help me with the words?'

27. Play with a tea set – make a cup of tea, pretend it is hot, then wash up afterwards!

28. If your child is a fussy eater, play a game of turn-taking at mealtime: 'My turn to eat a piece of carrot, now your turn.' You can use wet foods like yoghurt to make handprints, or dry food like pasta and popcorn to make bracelets, necklaces, and pictures. Again, hide toys in cereals or rice for them to find.

29. Play with bath toys at bath time – count the toys/what sound does the duck make? Read special waterproof books in the bath.

30. Jenga now comes in other materials other than wooden blocks, which is better for little ones. This is a great way to practise turn-taking.

31. Play with bath bubbles – generate language through lots of bubbles/soft bubbles/bubbles

flying up/bubbles in the bath/bubbles on the bath/bubbles on my head.

32. A dressing/undressing game offers a choice of items to put on next – vest or pants, pyjama top, or pyjama bottoms. You can have fun by getting them to put the clothes on in the wrong order, or socks on their hands.

33. Practise turn-taking writing the first letter of your child's name. You can do this on paper/dry sand/paint/shaving foam (if you are feeling brave!)

34. Take turns practising self-help skills – putting socks on/putting on coats/shoes. Tell your child to watch you, then they should try. Help them when struggling but let them try first. This will help with attention: are they able to stay to practise the skill?

35. When out for a walk or in the car – 'Let us count all the trees we can see.' 'How many red cars will we see on our way to the stores?'

36. Lay the table at mealtimes – 'I will lay out the plates and knives and you can lay out the spoons and forks.' Or, lay the table while they aren't watching, and leave one piece off each setting. See if they can spot the missing object.

37. Put the washing away – 'You put Daddy's socks in the drawer, and I will put my dress

away.' 'You put your socks in your drawer and I will hang your shirt.'

38. Watch TV together – the boy is sleeping/running/jumping/crying (building action words/verbs). It's important that you are commenting on what you are watching and asking children about what they can see.

39. Play 'Pass the Facial Expression'. This works well if you have siblings who want to play too. Sit in a circle and smile, then pass the smile on to your child, who has to pass it on to the next person. This is excellent for eye contact.

40. Play hopscotch – encourage waiting for their turn.

41. Play skittles/ten pin bowling – take turns (you can use empty plastic bottles and a ball).

42. Draw a familiar picture together. E.g., a man: 'You draw an eye, and I will draw an ear.'

43. Play 'Simon Says' – 'Simon says "Jump three times"'. Encourage your child to be 'Simon' – help them if they are not able to do it by themselves.

44. Thread large beads on a string to make a necklace.

45. Dice games like snakes and ladders.

46. Create a memory tray. Put various objects on a tray (how many will depend on their age). Give them a set amount of time to look at the objects

and then take it away. See how many they can remember.

47. Play football, taking turns to see who can kick the ball furthest away.

48. 'I spy with my little eye.' Start/teach the game by putting some items in front of your child, saying the names first, then starting the game. You can take the game outside once your child is familiar with the game and can generate words.

49. Get dressed together: 'Your turn to put a sock on, now my turn to put my sock on,' etc.

50. Make a post box out of a shoebox (cover the shoe box base and lid with some red paper, then cut out a hole a bit bigger than letter-size in the lid). Cut out pictures of animals/clothes/foods and take turns to post them in the post box. Open the box, take cards out, do the activity again, or swap another set of cards. Your child will learn new vocabulary in a fun way. Also, they will learn to wait for their turn. Your child will love learning whilst having lots of attention from you and having fun!!

51. Musical instruments – put two sets of three different musical instruments (you can use things from home that might make a noise; e.g., rice, pasta or dry beans in a plastic

bottle/pot and spoon for a drum/empty packet of crisps to make a crackling noise). Sit in front of your child and tell them to do 'good sitting' and 'good listening' and 'good looking' (if another adult is available, then they could sit with your child to support them with listening). Put the three instruments in front of you and three same instruments in front of your child. Practise playing each instrument – this will help your child become familiar with the sound each instrument makes. Start the game and tell your child, 'I am going to play one instrument; you wait, watch, and then copy me after I stop.' If your child copies by playing the same instrument as you did, then move to the next. If not, then play the same instrument again and encourage them to watch carefully and copy. When your child can successfully do this face-to-face game, then turn around with your back to your child and say: 'I am going to play an instrument, but you must listen because you will not be able to see what I am playing.' Do as above.

52. Symbolic noises – have a few different toy animals; e.g., dog, cat, duck, and do the same as the musical instruments game. If you do not have the toy animals, you can draw each animal on a different piece of paper and place

them in front of your child and you. They can then pick up the piece of paper when you make the animal noise, and you can do the same when your child does that.

53. Sing nursery rhymes – explain to your child that you are going to sing a familiar nursery rhyme, but that you do not remember all the words – 'Can you help me?!' Give reminders for 'good listening' and start the nursery rhyme together (make sure your child knows the song). You sing the first line, then pretend to forget the words – e.g., 'Twinkle, twinkle little star, how I wonder...' If your child continues singing, then join in with a few words later. Give specific praise; e.g., 'You did good listening'!! 'Thank you for helping, I forgot the words' (use a different tone of voice and facial expressions to make the activity exciting for your child).

54. Listening game; walk from room to room and encourage your child to 'listen', and help if they do not understand what they need to do. You might hear the 'humming' of the fridge, the ticking sound of the clock, the washing machine noise, or even their baby sister/brother crying! At the end, sit together and talk about how many things they heard. Say, 'Wow, you heard so many things, you did

brilliant listening!' (with a thumbs up). Encourage your child to imitate some of the noises they heard.

55. For older children, you could write down the names of the things they were able to hear and talk about them at the end – you can count how many different sounds you heard. Make it sound exciting, so that your child will want to join in the activity and feels this is their important time with you.

56. Listening games outside the home – say, 'We are going for a walk outside. Let's see what type of noises we can hear. We will make a list and talk about them when we get back home.' Talk about what noises they can expect to hear; e.g., a car, birds singing, dogs barking, buzzing bees, children playing/talking, etc.

57. Make symbolic animal sounds (cat, dog, lion) or vehicles (airplane, car), depending on the age and the ability of your child. You can always start but if your child finds the task difficult, make it simpler, and if they find it too easy, make it a little more difficult – but always make it fun and NOT like work!

58. Make daily boring tasks fun like loading/unloading the dishwasher, washing machine or tumble dryer, folding clothes, putting them away in different drawers, setting

up the table at mealtimes!! (If you have time –
otherwise, use short play activity.)

59. Make playdough. A simple recipe is 8 tbsp
flour, 2 tbsp salt, 1 tbsp of oil, 60ml of warm
water, and food colourings. Make shapes and
count your shapes.

60. Hanging clothes out on the washing line. Ask
your child to 'Pass me the red shirt/Daddy's
shirt/Mummy's socks/your trousers.'

61. Putting away the cutlery (be careful). Can they
count all the spoons/forks? Ask your child to
dry the different cutlery beforehand.

62. Get out in the garden. Plant seeds, and water
them together. Find different insects or use
sand moulds in the earth.

63. Tidying up: 'Let us see who can pick up more
things off the floor. Let's count!' Let your child
win and say, 'Wow, you win!!'

64. Putting the shopping away: ask your child to
pass you the cheese/apples/juice/milk, etc.,
(always start with 'Mummy needs help!')

65. Make a game of filling or emptying the
washing machine. You can take turns to put in
or take out each item of clothing. Say, 'It's your
turn to take out one thing; now it's my turn.' It
will take longer to complete the activity, but
your child will love spending this quality time

with you and this mundane work activity will hopefully be fun even for you!!

66. Baking: ask your child to add some of the ingredients or ask them to stir with the spoon. Take turns in stirring.

67. Help to write the shopping list – both of you look in the fridge/kitchen and see what you need to buy. If your child is not able to write, they can draw a picture of the item.

68. When in the stores, ask your child to tell you what you need to buy, and help them read out the shopping list.

69. Dusting – children love using the duster. 'You dust the table, and I will dust the TV/sofa/fan/bookcase/computer.'

70. Action map: draw an action map for your child to follow. Write 'START', then draw and write various actions like 'hop three times', 'say the alphabet', 'jump over the bridge' (make sure you draw the bridge!), 'walk ten steps', 'skip', 'count to 10', etc. for your child as they move along the path. Make the task as easy or as difficult according to your child's skills. If you are targeting attention and listening, make sure you write in a few pauses/stops on the map. For turn-taking, tell your child, 'You will take a turn, then me,' or their brother or sister will be taking a turn. Your child can help you

by telling you when to 'stop' and when to 'go' during the game. This will help your child to focus on their 'adult-like role' rather than becoming upset if they do not want you or their sibling to take a turn! You can stop the activity when the timer goes off and say, 'All finished', OR if your child is enjoying the activity, then you can continue.

71. Let your child do your hair and makeup. Label the items they are using and where to use them. For example, lipstick on Mummy's lips/blusher on the cheeks/clips in the hair.

72. Make puppets out of old socks. Make up stories and adventures for the puppets.

73. Counting game – when walking along the road, say, 'Let's see how many red cars we can see driving past.'

Use visual prompts such as pictures, objects, natural gestures like pointing and a range of facial expressions and tone of voice to get your child's interest.

Keep the activity short; use an egg timer to help your child to stay focused for a set time.

Talk about and model (show) these skills with your child: 'good waiting', 'good listening', 'good looking', 'good sitting', 'good turn-taking'.

Frequently give positive feedback even outside the 'playtime'.

Conclusion

In summary, child language development is complicated yet amazingly simple. This is probably the reason why I am so fascinated by it. Research shows that children need time to develop each skill at a certain age. However, they can make significant progress when offered a supportive environment. Children require love, attention and support from adults in their environment to thrive. You can provide all of these and more when you take some time to play with them, but more importantly, they are reaping the benefits of your wonderful speech and language example.

Spend time with your child on a one-to-one basis wherever possible and make it fun and memorable. Quite often, we assume this time has to be sat down in the living room but really, five minutes of quality time can be anywhere. If you have to wait for a sibling after an after-school activity, you can take advantage of this to play a game. Traffic is a huge pet hate for me and pretty much everyone; use it to play games like 'Eye Spy'.

Remember, children learn by watching you. Make sure when you are together you are modelling the skills you want your child to learn. Remember, children do as we do and not as we say!!

We have said that you should try to find time when it is just the two of you. That being said, if there is another spare five minutes in the day and they have older siblings, it is great to get them involved. There is often no greater idol and role model than a big brother or sister.

Now that you have learned how children learn each of the early interaction skills and why they need to develop these, you will feel confident in helping your child to develop these skills. Many times, you don't need a degree to give your child the best start possible. Even if your child's skills are not delayed, you can still use this book and especially the ideas for the games to build a positive relationship with your child. You now also know how and where to seek professional help if required. Don't feel as if you have failed if you do need to get help. The strategies are simple, and the theory is simple, but there are often extremely complex interactions that happen in the brain and it takes a trained specialist to get to the bottom of the issues.

You can play these games with more than one child. If you have two or three children of a similar age, make the game into a group game. I love the idea of a play date with specific games to target speech and language development. Let's face it, once one child is covered in shaving foam, or there are painted handprints all over your floors, you may as well have a blast with a few more little ones. This will also really help with social interactions. Plus, you will get the reputation of being the cool parents that do fun things (but remember – it's not a competition!).

Finally, don't forget to be a good language role model. Be patient and persevere and most importantly, have fun! I am confident that when you start to see small improvements, you are going to really love providing such amazing support to your little ones.

If you have found this book helpful and the games fun to do, then please take a few minutes to leave a review on Amazon. I also love to hear how you are all getting on. Thank you :)

Resources

1. Andrews, A. A., Corbett, T. C., Edwards, S. E., Royall, L. R., & Sharp, J. S. (2003–2004). *Attention Skills*. Mind. https://www.termpaperwarehouse.com/essay-on/Attention-Skills/183843.

2. cdc.gov. 2020. *Active Listening | Communicating | Essentials | Parenting Information | CDC*. [online] Available at: <https://www.cdc.gov/parents/essentials/communication/activelistening.html> [Accessed 11 September 2020].

3. Core Vocabulary. 2020. *Core Vocabulary*. [online] Available at: <http://corevocabulary.weebly.com/#> [Accessed 12 September 2020].

4. Culatta, R. C. (2020). *Social Development Theory*. instructionaldesign.org. https://www.instructionaldesign.org/theories/social-development.

5. Encyclopaedia of Children's Health. (n.d.). *Language Development.* Retrieved August 29, 2020, from http://www.healthofchildren.com/l/language -development.html.

6. https://audiology-speech.com/expressive-language/.

7. *Importance of attention in early communication development.* (2020). Mind. https://mindinstitutes.com/the-importance-of-attention-in-early-communication-development/.

8. McLeod, S. A. (2018, June 06). *Jean Piaget's theory of cognitive development.* Simply Psychology. https://www.simplypsychology.org/piaget.html.

9. McLeod, S. A. (2018, August 05). *Lev Vygotsky.* Simply Psychology. https://www.simplypsychology.org/vygotsky.html.

10. National Literacy Trust. 2020. *10 Reasons Why Play Is Important | National Literacy*

Trust. [online] Available at:
<https://literacytrust.org.uk/resources/10-reasons-why-play-important/#:~:text=%20Here%20are%2010%20reasons%20why%20it%20is,the%20truck%20on%20the%20ground%20but...%20More%20> [Accessed 11 September 2020].

11. Nottingham Children's Speech and Language Therapy. (n.d.). *Attention levels and Strategies.* Cooper, Moodley and Reynell. Retrieved September 5, 2020, from https://www.nottinghamshirehealthcare.nhs.uk/download.cfm?doc=docm93jijm4n2488.pdf&ver=2709.

12. Provide. (n.d.). Children's Services Information Sheet, Blank Levels of Questioning. PSI-3718C-2028-01. www.provide.org.uk.

13. *Understanding Language.* (2020). Kid Sense. https://childdevelopment.com.au/areas-of-concern/understanding-language/#:~:text=Understanding%20of%20language%20(also%20known,to%20understand%20words%20and%20language.

CPSIA information can be obtained
at www.ICGtesting.com
Printed in the USA
BVHW031218120722
641924BV00004BA/439

9 781914 261053